PLATFORM PAPERS

**QUARTERLY ESSAYS ON THE PERFORMING ARTS
FROM CURRENCY HOUSE**

**No. 59
May 2019**

CURRENCY HOUSE

Platform Papers Partners

Platform Papers
Readers' Forum

Readers' responses to our previous essays are posted on our website. Contributions to the conversation (250 to 2000 words) may be emailed to info@currencyhouse. org.au. The Editor welcomes opinion and criticism in the interest of healthy debate but reserves the right to monitor where necessary.

Platform Papers, quarterly essays on the performing arts, is published every February, May, August and November and is available through bookshops, by subscription and online in paper or electronic version. For details see our website at www.currencyhouse.org.au.

NGARRA-BURRIA*:
New music and the search for an Australian sound

||||||||||||||||||||||||||||||||||||||||||||||||||||||||||||||||||||||||||

CHRISTOPHER SAINSBURY

Ngarra-burria means 'to listen, to sing' in the Dharug language of Sydney

ABOUT THE AUTHOR

Dr Christopher Sainsbury is an Australian Indigenous composer and performer, and a descendant of Australia's first settled Aboriginal people—the *Dharug* (also known as *Eora*). The steel-string guitar is his main instrument and he maintains an active career as a guitarist performing jazz, contemporary and new music styles. He articulates his heritage through his work, and has done so since the mid-1980s. He grew up on the Central Coast and returns there frequently.

For some 35 years he has made a steady contribution to Australian music as a working composer in both professional and community music arenas. His works range from large instrumental and vocal works to children's songs, jazz to folk, and chamber works. His influences include the Australian composer James Penberthy and musicians as varied as American bassist and composer Steve Swallow, and German composer Hans Werner Henze. Jazz and surf music are also influences, and the Australian band Taman Shud.

As a student in 1986 Sainsbury won the Young Australian Composer Award and the College Medal from the Northern Rivers College of Advanced Education. He was commissioned in 1988 by the Australian Chamber Orchestra for his *Homage to*

TS Eliot. In 1994 his incidental music for the play *Aboriginal Protestors* was featured at the Sydney Festival and the Weimar Festival. His *Concerto for Guitar* written for Spanish virtuoso Jose Maria Gallardo Del Rey was commissioned for the Darwin International Guitar Festival 2002; and in 2004 his work *My Eye Has Seen My Desire* was toured by renowned Nederlands ensemble Duo Bosgraaf-Elias. In 2010 his orchestral work *First Light* won an international scores competition hosted and performed by the New England Philharmonic Orchestra, Boston, USA.

His compositions draw upon sounds from his 'aural homelands' of Sydney and the Central Coast. Among many commissions has been one from Primal Dance Company for their modern ballet work *Scar Tree* (for the Sydney Fringe Festival and East Coast Tour), and another from former Senator Bob Brown to arrange his *The Earth Song* for community choir and performance at Canberra Writers' Festival 2016. His recent commissioners are the Friends of Chopin Australia for pianist Edward Neeman (2018) and a new work for the Canberra International Music Festival conducted by Roland Peelman (2019). A recent international performance has been by the Yale Concert Band (USA) in 2019. His narrative-based work *Bark of the 'bidgee* is commissioned by the Canberra International Music Festival.

Sainsbury is also a committed educator and was music teacher and/or Head of Arts and Media 1990–2015 at the Eora College. He has also taught at UTS and at

Avondale College. His work with other Indigenous musicians has resulted in several major APRA grants 2016–18 for the Indigenous Composer Initiative (now known as *Ngarra-burria*: First Peoples Composers) in which he works closely with Moogahlin Performing Arts, Redfern.

In his long-term home on the Central Coast he was director of a large community choir. He has also been musical director for many Aboriginal theatre and music events in Redfern including Sydney's first Koorabaret in 1992. His own group A Band Called Bouddi (1992–96) performed his song cycle based on a lecture by Dr David Suzuki which was premiered at the UNSW Environmental Symposium. He has performed his own compositions from his solo guitar CD *Anima* at venues around Australia. His website is www.sainsburymusic.com

Acknowledgements

I would like to thank Liza-Mare Syron and Katharine Brisbane who initiated the idea of this paper. Thanks also to both for extensive comments and assistance in the development of the paper. Without them there would be no Platform Paper 59. Thanks also to Michael Campbell who helped me through the period of wanting to toss it, and settling my mind.

Thanks to my wife Christina Sainsbury for her generous support and for believing in me. What a blessing. To my Indigenous family and community in Sydney and the Central Coast, thank you. I'd also like to acknowledge and thank the late Jimmy Little and also Darryl Griffen, for walking with me in Indigenous music development at the Eora Centre. I also remember many of the local guitarists from Redfern and thank them for their music, especially Lachy, Hotshot and Tommy (all deceased).

I must acknowledge Kim Cunio, Frank Millward and Bonnie McConnell from the School of Music at the ANU who have encouraged me over this past year to 'write it up'. Also thank you to Malcolm Gillies for his keen eye and support along the way, and for believing in my voice and style, and to Royston Gustavson for initially committing the School of Music to support the *Ngarra-Burria* initiative.

Thanks to our composer mentors Kevin Hunt, Kim Cunio and Deborah Cheetham. You've truly gone above and beyond. Deborah, you're an inspiration. Thanks also to First Peoples USA (Mohican) composer Brent Michael Davids, as you too inspire me.

Thanks to our lead partner Moogahlin Performing Arts who is our 'cultural mothership', especially Fred Copperwaite and Lily Shearer. You are always there to inspire. You create pathways for us. Lily, thanks for the whole Brewarrina trip. Thanks also to Ally Murphy-Oates for Moogahlin administration support, without which there would be no Ngarra-burria.

Thanks to the Australian Music Centre, and especially I thank John Davis, for his belief in and support for the program. You've always been there for us, as friend and advisor. To Claire Edwards and Ensemble Offspring, you turned it into sound. Thank you for energising the vision that we shared, and expanding it. It's been a great, a genuine two-way collaboration. Thanks to APRA for their generous support, and particularly Michael Hutchings. Thanks to Beth Ridgeway, Jasmine Robertson, Dallas Wellington and Gabby DiNallo from the Eora Centre. Your valuable in-kind support and friendship has really enabled us.

Thanks to Lt Steven Stanke and Lt Brian O'Kane from the Royal Australian Navy Band for making a serious commitment to us this year.

Lastly I thank the composers. Your wealth of musical and cultural experience humbles me in leading this program.

1: 'When did you discover you were Aboriginal?'

I am an Aboriginal Australian of mixed heritage (that includes Irish, Dutch and also English) and this places me in an unusual position as a composer of new music[1] in our country. As a fair-skinned *Koori* person, often I have to navigate common misunderstandings around my heritage and identity. Whilst the expectation to contribute as an Indigenous person is welcome, at times it is also a weight to bear.

My grandfather was a handsome brown man, and I still envy his skin tone. He was born in the 1910s in Yass and the family moved to Sydney in the 1920s.[2] He was 'very well assimilated'. With regard to most Sydney Aboriginals, the assimilation policy of the NSW Aboriginal Welfare Board[3] (established 1940) had been in de facto effect to some extent since Governor Macquarie's Parramatta Native Institution (established 1813), and later his Blacktown Native Institution (BNI).[4] Through that initiative children were being removed, teenagers pressed into service, and later young adults were being encouraged to marry convicts. Assimilation was a practice of whole integration into the new culture. So the policy of 1940 simply coupled with a previous modus operandi, which was certainly the Sydney Aboriginals' experience. Being wholly integrated wasn't completely our family's experience, but close.

Further relating to my background, pertaining to the term for the Aboriginal people and language of Sydney, there exist a few views.[5] Some call the Sydney people and their language *Dharug*, others *Eora*, among a few other terms. Some say that *Eora* is the coastal dialect of the inland *Dharug* speakers, around Western Sydney. The boundaries of the Sydney people are also a matter for debate. I can contribute only a little to this, from what I know best—music. As a composer I am a deep listener. I suggest that Daramulan, son of the local Creator Spirit Baiame, sounds his name within neighbouring languages— *Darkingjung* to the north-west of Sydney, *Dharug* in Sydney (or Western Sydney), and *Darawal* to the south of Sydney—as all carry the *'Dar'* or *'Dara'* sound. I hear it as integral, and I hear it in *Dharug*. It's all I can offer, and any more is for history scholars. I refer to myself as a *Dharug* person—a people whose coastal dialect in more recent times has been referred to as 'the *Eora*'. I grew up on the Central Coast to the north of Sydney, and am aware that the country as far north as Terrigal in my home region was also termed *Dharug*.[6]

Jumping ahead, from 1990 I worked at the Eora Centre for Aboriginal Visual and Performing Arts,[7] Redfern. There, while I was still rather young, various community members and elders associated with the centre encouraged me greatly in my heritage and identity. One of these was the veteran singer and entertainer

Jimmy Little.[8] He took me aside one day shortly after I'd started, and said: 'We've all got our part to play, and in our own way we have to make our contribution, and that is what makes community.' He talked of the responsibilities that came with being experienced Indigenous musicians—essentially giving back. His acknowledgement of me, and his investment of time, meant a great deal to me.

I do not say that I identify as Aboriginal, but that I am Aboriginal, like the artist Brenda Croft, who states: 'I foreground my Aboriginality.' She affirms this even though she acknowledges her other heritage.[9] The Aboriginals of Sydney have long been engrossed by other people's perceptions of their heritage and identity. In an essay from the mid-1990s, Dr Denis Byrne wrote about how in the early settlement of Sydney, for the Europeans 'the natives were fast losing that quality of being [...] authentically primitive'.[10] Today, Indigenous academic, author, actor and theatre director Dr Liza-Mare Syron suggests that even some [Indigenous people] will 'validate [one's identity], while others may not'.[11]

Bringing it back to music and to my personal experience, in 2010 a relatively young Sydney composer and academic[12] asked me: 'When did you discover you were Aboriginal?' I highlight it as an example of a not-too-infrequent question from non-Indigenous people to some fair-skinned *Kooris*, and even to non-fair-skinned *Kooris*. I discussed this incident with Aboriginal composer Deborah Cheetham, and both she and I agree that it's the wrong question, and should not be asked.

3

Was this person looking to ascertain a certain level of authenticity of my Indigeneity? Were they articulating the aforementioned 1800s European notion of authenticity? Either way, I don't entertain such discussions, and feel that it further sustains the legacy of assimilation by dividing Indigenous people as half-castes, quadroons, octoroons and even those who didn't know. Yet, as Jimmy pointed out to me, I had a part to play. Teaching at the Eora Centre was a part of that.

The Eora Centre and a New Music initiative

Darryl Griffen—Aboriginal musician and an exschoolteacher—took up the College Director's position at Eora in 2000. By that time I was the Head of Arts and Media at the Centre. Darryl and I had known each other for some time. Together we explored the idea of a performance company attached to the College, to serve the music and theatre graduates and assist them to emerge into industry. But ultimately the core business of the day-to-day teaching kept all at Eora busy, and given the additional costs that the project would have incurred, it never eventuated. So unlike the Black Theatre, we were an accredited Indigenous tertiary centre, but not a company. It still runs as such.

Since my own college years[13] I'd maintained a music practice as well as teaching. At Eora I shared my experience with students—writing for small scratch ensembles and staging concerts at the centre and in community venues. It was meaningful to me to bring my composition and teaching skills together in this way. At times we co-wrote small pieces. Very early on, I was delighted (not surprised), to see that many other Indigenous musicians could write much more broadly than rock, reggae or country music (although there was plenty of that too). Some theatre shows included music scored by students and myself, and there was the occasional new music concert.[14] As well some students wrote soundtracks to short films being made by the film students. This was in the period 1990–94.[15] The talent was there, and the other music staff and I had heard much that was 'left-of-centre'—more along the composed line, and worth fostering. That early groundswell lives on in new manifestations, of which the *Ngarra-burria*: First Peoples Composers program is a part.

In December of 2014 I approached John Davis, the CEO of the Australian Music Centre (AMC) about setting up a mechanism to support Indigenous composers, for there were a few with a profile and potentially many others. He quickly agreed that this was something that the AMC should be a part of, and we discussed an operational template. This included: what Indigenous organisations, what other partners, might become involved; which Indigenous composers could be mentors; other relevant mentors; potential Indigenous composers who could be in the program; what the program might look like; what the program's aims might be; what might our composers want from the program; what the program might cost; where to find funding—and more. In 2016 we secured funding to begin the program—the Indigenous Composers Initiative—the first name for the program, and the name under which it ran from late 2016 to late 2018.

After two years, late in 2018, Fred Copperwaite, co-artistic director of our cultural advisory and organisational partner, Moogahlin Performing Arts, suggested we needed a brand that was in essence Indigenous. Moogahlin is an Indigenous performing arts company based in the Carriageworks contemporary multi-arts centre in Sydney.[16] They support Indigenous performing artists—theatre, music and cross-disciplinary included—and Indigenous youth performance, and are the leading Indigenous theatre company in New South Wales.

A number of individuals from our partners (listed below) proposed various names and ultimately we agreed on '*Ngarra-burria*: First Peoples Composers', drawing upon my language as the founder of the program and also placing it firmly in Sydney where it started. Many of those involved had studied or worked at the Eora Centre in Redfern and Chippendale[17] at some stage in the last 30 years, so the local language of Sydney was relevant.[18]

The following is taken from the Australian Music Centre's website, and presents concise information on what the program is about. It was originally written by John Davis and myself, and will serve to briefly introduce the reader to the composers—a major focus of this paper.

In 2016, the Australian Music Centre, together with [partners] Moogahlin Performing Arts, APRA AMCOS grants funding, the Australian National University School of Music and Ensemble Offspring,[19] launched a new initiative aimed at supporting emerging Aboriginal and Torres Strait Islander composers in new music and jazz. A part of the AMPlify framework of artist develop-ment programs, the pilot stage of the Indigenous Composer Initiative took place in NSW and the ACT over [late] 2016 and 2017.

The AMPlify Indigenous Composer Initiative aims at helping artists in establishing contacts, networks and relationships with role models, and engaging in knowledge exchange and learning. The focus of the initiative is to identify Indigenous composers not yet properly represented or heard across new art music and jazz, and support them in creating works of new Indigenous music in score format. This in turn will help to create new opportunities, in new contexts, for Indigenous people: e.g. performance in new music events, schools repertoire, examination syllabi pieces, etc.

Five invited participants—Rhyan Clapham, Brenda Gifford, Tim Gray, Troy Russell and Elizabeth Sheppard—took part in the initiative in 2016-2017, and the same participants later went on to take part in the 2018 edition of the program. In 2016-2017, each artist worked on several compositions for voice and/or small ensemble. Facilitators for the pilot project included composer Christopher Sainsbury and jazz pianist, composer and educator Kevin Hunt.

The Indigenous Composer Initiative concert [for 2017] took place at the Eora College in Sydney on 3 August 2017. You can listen to the performances and composer interviews as part of ABC Classic FM's New Waves podcast and view the program and read program notes by participating artists.[20]

In the remainder of this paper I shall explore Australian composers' fascination with an Australian sound, and the referencing of Indigenous music, stories, themes and narratives in their works. I will also share my experience getting to know the new music sector: the need for, and the unique distinction of, the *Ngarra-burria*: First Peoples Composers program, and any consistent themes streaming through the compositions of the composers involved. I will highlight real or potential issues around Indigenous composers emerging into the art music scene in Australia. Much of this is necessarily political, and also goes into some musical analysis—yet is always related to an Indigenous cultural context. *Ngarra-burria* is still negotiating its way.

We have seen a great deal of interest emerging around the program, and commitment to the program. We're young, yet old. Ultimately it's not about the music, but about the cultures of which the music is an expression. Lastly, I suggest ways of working with Indigenous composers, what's working and what we can do better in the various branches of the 'classical' or new music industry, and show ways forward that hopefully can serve as ideas for strategic planning and real action.

2: Australian composers and the search for an Australian sound

In 1991 Sounds Australia's publication *The Composer Speaks* (ed. Graeme Skinner) published a record of a debate held at the Australian National Composers' Conference in Sydney in 1988. Its title was 'That Australian Composers Should Set Out to Develop a Distinctive Australian Music'.[21] Such a debate had existed long before and was seen as a legitimate inquiry, with which all countries with a history of colonisation must grapple in their search to understand their origins and their community.

However, I sense that amongst Australian Indigenous composers a 'distinctive Australian music' is not something with which we are, or have been, overly concerned. It is more accepted that this is inherent. Instead, Indigenous composers articulate stories, themes and narratives from their/our cultures. This may be stories of place and belonging, stories pertaining to Indigenous spirituality, historical experiences since colonisation, family or clan stories, and certain aspects from narratives and issues that are thrust upon us, or that arise from within our communities.[22] As most now know, some of this is not pleasant. Yet many Indigenous people (including some of our composers) live with it.

In the context of the then debate, Australian composer Richard Mills has stated: 'The problem of espousing too strongly the cause of a distinctive Australian music can get lost in superficial gesture.' He was referring directly to the practice by some composers of adorning our music with elements of other cultures (or 'paraphernalia' as he called it)—citing Aboriginal and Asian music materials.[23]

In the same debate English-born composer Roger Smalley spoke of hearing 'melody with a modal basis, [being] a very strong thread running through a great deal of Australian music'. He added: 'I also think that simple repetitive rhythms are a characteristic of Australian music.'[24]

It is important to hear from one such as Smalley, coming from further afield. Such informed newcomers can unpack aspects of what we're doing locally, and give it global comparison, ascertaining whether we have something distinctive, perhaps even an Australian accent or voice through our collective music. What particularly appeals to me as a composer is that Smalley also stated: 'There is a lack of thoroughgoing, elaborate, symphonic kind of development in Australian music.'[25]

Although he was wrong—listen to Penberthy, Douglas, Mills, even Michael Kieran Harvey (as composer)—I loved it! Through this statement he enabled me. Over time I had come to realise that the dominant European tradition in music composition emphasised far too weightily its own aesthetics, and I wasn't wholly happy with it. Its arena is one of entitlement, and it still dictates, 'Be schooled thus.' Here in the Antipodes, Australian music has followed this dictate with eagerness, and we're still largely cut from their cloth—the Europeans. It is as if on the one hand we've been espousing an Australian music, yet on the other we've been happily chained to some of Europe's best (and sadly, worst) music. Let others speak as to why. As for me, in large part I've managed to walk in a parallel world to that of classical and modern European music. Perhaps it was living up the coast outside of our major cities and centring my work on local expressions.[26] Perhaps it was working in community—at Eora—or maybe it was simply my instrument, the steel-string guitar, which is not a part of the classical world. Nevertheless, when I was young I trained well in that world, worked in that world, and had some noted successes.[27] Yet I noticed in myself that walking away from it always felt far better for me than walking towards it. Finally, around thirty years of age, I dropped any association with it. Quite quickly I became an unknown, even to the few who had known me in the past, and gladly so. Then it was like, 'Great, let the music begin!'[28]

Australian composers tripping over my Aboriginality

Over time I had noted that amongst some Australian composers my Aboriginality presented an issue. Four composers currently or historically associated with leading universities have demonstrated to me their ill-preparedness to engage with Indigenous people. Firstly I turn to Peter Sculthorpe.[29]

In 2002 Peter Sculthorpe and I were programmed to present compositions at the Darwin International Guitar Festival. He had a short and light chamber work steeped in a popular vein,[30] and I had a guitar concerto, written at the invitation of Festival Director Adrian Walter, for visiting Spanish virtuoso Jose Maria Gallardo del Rey. I'd only met Sculthorpe as a student.

The festival was a week of concerts, workshops, competitions, classes and socials. One afternoon he was alone and I introduced myself to him. We talked about a mutual friend, James Penberthy, a senior composer, who had since passed on and who had been my mentor. He enjoyed remembering Jim and we had quite a bit to share for a while. Then at some point I positioned myself and changed the subject. 'Do you know any Aboriginal composers?' I asked. He didn't. I then confided my Aboriginality, confident that, given his history of referencing Aboriginal music materials and concepts, themes and narratives in his works, that we would have an enjoyable conversation. I assumed that he would understand the importance to me of my heritage and identity. But he simply replied: 'Really? You don't look it.' I was shocked. Whilst it was dismissive, I don't believe it was intended to be rude. We talked for a little while longer. Soon I walked away from this elder statesman of Australian music, thinking: 'In terms of Indigenous cultural awareness this fellow needs up-skilling.'

In the late 1990s I enrolled for a Master's degree in Music at the Sydney Conservatorium of Music, University of Sydney, and in 2009 for a PhD. I had a family and a full-time job, and never got to the Conservatorium much. That suited me, as often when I went there I wondered, 'Why am I doing this?' I was ready to engage with new music again, but on my terms, not willy-nilly emulating Europe's best and worst. I came up with an approach. This was that I would take it (new music) down to the shores of the local lake where I lived on the Central Coast, bury it and see what grew from there. It is a metaphor for taking any new knowledge home, and living with it in my context, rather than me adapting my music to its context. I don't think this was just an Aboriginal thing, more the need of a middle-ageing composer. It aided me in finding who I am in this world of new music.

During my studies another notable composer and academic[31] encouraged me on the one hand to express my Aboriginality through my music, yet on the other hand corrected me with: 'But you're not an Aboriginal, you are a person of Aboriginal heritage.' I was a little bewildered, not offended, but maintained my course.

On another occasion, yet another composer academic inquired: 'So you identify as Aboriginal?' I turned it around and replied: 'My Aboriginality identifies in me.' This is another question that Deborah Cheetham and I agree should not be asked by non-Indigenous people. It can be polarising. The person concerned was not being rude, just ill-prepared in matters pertaining to Aboriginal identity. Then, during one group session I observed a lecturer advising: 'Aboriginal people do not hear counterpoint.' They were suggesting they had knowledge of 'traditional Indigenous music', but they should have known that even here complex counterpoints arise, in some ways like Ligeti's micro-polyphony. It serves as a further example of the general lack of knowledge of Aboriginal people, their heritage and their expressions of identity, which are many. It was becoming apparent to me that perceptions of Indigenous identity by some of our non-Indigenous composers and academics were not aligned with Indigenous ways of expressing identity.

Sector interest in authentic Indigenous content

Today many of our academics, composers, commissioning ensembles, music organisations, programmers and broadcasters are saying 'yes' to Indigenous content, as is evidenced by programming, yet I sense they still prefer the more 'authentic or traditional' end of the spectrum. Perhaps it articulates a need for connecting with what they perceive to be authentic cultures. Yet are they? Are not fair-skinned *Kooris* or those from the south-eastern states also authentic? Without dismissing other Indigenous peoples, at present I see few of them/ us in these collaborations or programs. And many musical organisations still default to the work of known non-Indigenous composers working with Indigenous music. For instance, I heard Sculthorpe's *Djilile* (string orchestra version) performed by the Australian Chamber Orchestra again in recent months.

Indigenous composer Deborah Cheetham, her Short Black Opera Company, and the *Ngarra-burria* program are raising a flag about local Indigenous people and content, and music organisations have an opportunity to shift with us. In 2019 there should be no need to ask why. Most of the *Ngarra-burria* composers are only now recognising the assumed and free use of Indigenous materials and culture by some non-Indigenous compos-ers over the years. They will make comment in their own time. It is true that Deborah and I have a musical language that is largely Western; and that some people expect Aboriginal music to carry aspects of our tradi-tional music; but our themes and expressions are often very much born of Aboriginal experience. We are not trying to further authenticate our music.

Brent Michael Davids, a Mohican First Nations composer from the USA, has a unique voice, and is a very fine composer with many accolades, as exemplified through his work with one of the world's leading vocal groups, Chanticleer. He is one of the more significant composers of the 21st century. Davids organically sounds his traditions in much of his work, yet even where he doesn't, where a piece is more Western-sounding, he remains authentically a First Nations composer.

Given the misunderstandings here around Indigenous people and identity, I do find it stressful being an Indigenous composer in Australia. And I'm often more happy simply playing my steel-string guitar at a community event or gig, than working in the professional or community music composition arena. I'm very happy to fulfil 'my part' as Jimmy put it years ago, but he too enjoyed quiet moments.

At this stage I'd like to clearly outline the rationale for the *Ngarra-burria*: First Peoples Composers program. Firstly, there *are* Indigenous composers.

Besides Deborah Cheetham and myself—perhaps the first Indigenous Australian people to establish ourselves as composers—there is the master yidaki player William Barton, who, at the time of writing this paper, celebrates 20 years performing and composing; and Troy Russell, who has been composing for around 25 years. Troy recently found a second wind through the *Ngarra-burria* program. Clint Bracknell held full-time music positions at both the University of WA and Sydney University. Brenda Gifford, Elizabeth Sheppard and Tim Gray were a part of the first edition program. And *Ngarra-burria* composer Rhyan Clapham won the Create NSW Peter Sculthorpe Fellowship for 2018–19, an open and competitive scholarship. Then there was salon-style pianist-composer Roy Read, and composer David Page of the Bangarra Dance Company family, who have now passed on. This is simply to name some that I've known, ones who can really 'cut it' in the industry.[32] I am aware of others too, and many more emerging, such as violinist Eric Avery. But despite the public interest in Indigenous culture, most of us remain unheard. This is negligent, given the focus on, and esteem for, Indigenous culture. The fact that we are there is the first rationale for the *Ngarra-burria* program.

Next, I must point out that some non-Indigenous composers have occupied the Indigenous space. Many non-Indigenous composers have referenced Indigenous music, culture, themes or narratives in their compositions. At times, some have done so effectively, disempowering Indigenous composers. This has occurred for many decades. Can we imagine artists doing the same in the arts sector? A part of this is our lack of visibility. To correct this situation is also an incentive for the program.

Perhaps it is that some of us are perceived as less than authentic, and others not modern enough—too tonal or simplistic. And I know some Indigenous composers experience a tension between the expectations of the new music sector and those of their community. Academia and the new music sector readily dictate style and method to all developing composers; but for Indigenous composers, whether from Australia or elsewhere, such institutionalised entitlement needs to be brought into balance. It is true that Indigenous composers should learn the trade, but at present our cultural context is still being treated as amateurish, or less relevant than others. The dominant European traditions and expressions are still being upheld as the benchmark. This is not sustainable.

In 2016 I was present at the Sydney Opera House's one-off performance of Deborah Cheetham's opera *Pecan Summer*. Peter McCallum, long-term academic and music reviewer, was sitting behind me,[33] and after the event asked me how I liked it. 'Very, very much,' I replied. I must admit that I wondered where it placed him as a reviewer and whether he was reviewing that evening or not. The achievement of this event was much more than the question of the quality of the piece or of the performance, which were in any case excellent. Here was palpable community-making through performance. Aboriginal community was a force within the audience, who cheered and cried to see and hear their own on stage. This was from our story. This was from one of the most defining stories of Australia! I'd never witnessed a classical event that had achieved anything like *Pecan Summer*. My informed review was that it was a pinnacle of Australian music making over the past 50 years, and most missed it! Why was that? Once more, European traditions and expressions are institutionally preferred, whilst Indigenous artists are relegated to the periphery.

Indigenous themes in composition practice

Currently there are 60 composers listed on the Australian Music Centre's website who are influenced by 'Indigenous themes'. CEO John Davis states that there are actually many more.[34] An investigation of some of the works of these composers shows reference to Indigenous culture and history, and includes: music quotations, Indigenous words borrowed for titles, contemporary Indigenous issues explored, collaborations with Indigenous people, collaborations with non-Indigenous poets who utilise Indigenous themes, and more. These practices are something of a default position for some of our composers. I call such alignment with, or use of, Indigenous music, culture, themes or narratives 'Indigenous referencing'. And when used for a body of work I call it 'Indigenous posturing'.

I will now outline three leading composers' use of Indigenous music and aspects of culture, or themes and narratives. These are John Anthill, James Penberthy and Peter Sculthorpe. Firstly, let me establish that they were in fact non-Indigenous. Australian law states that to be Indigenous one must satisfy a three-tiered criterion:

- Indigenous heritage,
- personal identification as Indigenous,
- recognition as such by their community of origin or the community in which they live.[35]

I didn't know Anthill, but his pictorial modern work *Corroboree* was always presented as the composition of a non-Indigenous person who had been witness to a corroboree as a child. The work raises an interesting point. Various European composers in the early 20th century, including Bartok and Vaughan Williams, in various of their works had responded to the folk traditions of their peoples. Yet Indigenous music is not a folk tradition belonging to the modern Australian peoples. Anthill wrote events or scenes into his ballet score such as 'Witchetty-grub men with the emu totem people'. He was utilising aspects of Aboriginal life, albeit of his own invention. My mother-in-law was the Australian poet Isobel Robin, a keen Thomas Hardy scholar. I inherited a book from her unique collection, *Folkways in Thomas Hardy* by Ruth A. Firor, which has relevance to this discussion.[36] Reading both this book and Indigenous author Bruce Pascoe's *Dark Emu*[37] brings clarity to the fact that Firor's study of Essex folkways is far removed from Pascoe's outline of Australian 'Indigenism'.[38] Perhaps some of our composers have presumed folk music and Indigenous music to be the same, and indeed leading early- to mid-20th-century Australian composer Alfred Hill saw Indigenous music as a rich resource for our music composition. He wrote:

> *There is enough material in these recordings to start an entirely Australian school of music, as different in idiom as Vaughan Williams and the English School from anything else. It's a gold mine [...] All*

these young fellows who are composing now will have the chance of a lifetime with this material.[39]

Perhaps James Penberthy and also Peter Sculthorpe read this article in 1950.

I knew James Penberthy quite well, as his student.[40] At times James mentioned that he believed he had Indigenous heritage stemming from one of his grandmothers. He never validated it. In any case James did not identify as Indigenous, nor was he recognised by any community. He never understood my being Indigenous, and, when comparing me with other Indigenous peoples, referred to them as 'the real ones'. I let it go because I was young and not quite prepared to speak back to him, and because he was a man of his era.[41] In James Murdoch's book, *Australia's Contemporary Composers*,[42] Penberthy has more work listed under Indigenous themes than any other composer. He referenced Indigenous stories frequently, and in contrast to Hill he had met and spent time with many Indigenous people. Nevertheless, unlike many recent composers he did not really collaborate with them.

Peter Sculthorpe used Indigenous music and songs on many occasions. He not only referenced Indigenous music in new compositions, but also built a body of work around them. Jonathan Paget highlights:

Almost all of the Aboriginal melodies he has used have come from anthropological books and recordings—particularly the pioneering work of A.P.

Elkin, Trevor Jones and Jeremy Beckett, among others.[43]

To this end I will look at his piece *Djilile* later. The main point here is drawing Indigenous material from texts, not long-term engagement with Indigenous communities or song owners. As well as utilising actual Aboriginal music in some of his works, he emulated it, and in his String Quartet No.12: *From Ubirr* (1994) that stems in part from his 1986 work *Earth Cry*, he states as much. In this work he draws upon the timbres and resonances of Aboriginal traditional music, and simulates an Aboriginal melody very effectively. His works find favour within a quorum of art music listeners, music organisations, performers and programmers whose fascination with, and even esteem for, Indigenous culture further validate his music, without too much thought to any misuse of Indigenous materials. Nevertheless, I feel that amongst our composers, in Sculthorpe we had our 'Whitlam moment'—the one in which the Prime Minister ceremonially handed back a handful of sand to the Indigenous peoples of this land.[44]

Sculthorpe encouraged us to look to our First Peoples in order to find our place and identity as modern Australians. So, even though he dismissed my Aboriginality, I cannot deny him his depth and significance.

A few years prior to his passing, Sculthorpe disclosed to William Barton and others that he had recently discovered that he was of Indigenous heritage.[45] As far as I'm aware he himself never made this public. I know of two Sculthorpes who are indeed Indigenous, and also come from Sculthorpe's home state of Tasmania. Yet in the chat we had in Darwin in 2002 he told me that Indigenous people had married into his family, but that he was not from their bloodline. So some confusion exists at present. He may or may not have been of Indigenous heritage. What is clear is that he did not identify as Indigenous, nor did the Tasmanian or Sydney community where he lived acknowledge him as Indigenous. Therefore, under Australian law and according to Indigenous communities recognition practices, he was not.

Before exploring other examples I would like to highlight that for many Australian composers both our land and our Indigenous cultures remain a focus in their works. Smalley was hearing something of this. Effectively, many composers through their work sense and express our belonging to the Australian land and culture. It is an understandable focus. There have been many excursions by composers into Indigenous culture: some have been overreaching while engaging with Indigenous peoples; others have made more *'lite'* appro-priations.[46] In my music I also express the spirit of our land, yet usually pertaining to the context of one place or region—the Central Coast of NSW and Sydney—my long-term home and my aural homelands. Like other composers, I too look to Indigenous culture, yet with a decided focus on the local Aboriginal culture of the Central Coast and neighbouring Sydney, a culture of which I am a part, and that is a part of me. I don't know a wide brown land, or the desert, or the tropical north, but I do know the South-East, and my area within it.

While I don't endorse Indigenous referencing, I understand why it has been, and sometimes still is, a practice, for so many people are exploring the evolving Australian identity. As Australians we are negotiating who we are, our authenticity, our place. That's a great thing as it involves communities from all ethnicities and origins in Australia and the composers I discuss below are part of that. Yet today, borrowing aspects of Indigenous music or culture for a new work as a default position to suggest authenticity, is no longer needed. Most Indigenous people are unaware that it even goes on.

I am aware that some aspects of Indigenous culture and its expressions are already in the hands of the broader Australian public, effectively in the public domain. These may be place names, or the didgeridoo (yidaki) as an iconic image of Australia; and in the recent reclamation of language the co-branding of titles in national parks, civic centres, and arts buildings. As composers we need to know how to engage with all that, because it's not just words or 'stuff', it's from Indigenous culture. Even 'the songlines' are by default now owned by all Australians since the Bruce Chatwin novel of the same name.[47]

In the following examples I draw upon relevant information from the composers' scores, websites or the Australian Music Centre website.[48] It is all publicly available. They are all non-Indigenous composers.[49] These works exemplify their creator's use of Indigenous referencing or Indigenous posturing.

Example 1: Peter Sculthorpe's Maranoa Lullaby (orig. c1940s). This was originally an Aboriginal song from an area of Southern Queensland. Sculthorpe himself stated: 'When I was a student in Melbourne in the 1940s, I made an orchestral arrangement of the lullaby. I have since used it in several works, notably *Cello Dreaming* (1986).'[50] What is missing here is whether he had permission to use the song for his own creative works. As established above, he drew from anthropological texts and recordings.

Example 2: Peter Sculthorpe's Djilile for cello (1986). The composer stated it: 'is partly based on an adaptation of an Aboriginal melody collected in Arnhem Land in the late 50s by A. P. Elkin and Trevor Jones.'[51]

Example 3: Peter Sculthorpe's Dune Dreaming is movement five from *Great Sandy Island* (1998). It contains the word 'Dreaming', which seems harmless enough, and also describes 'falling pentatonic figures', which Sculthorpe has likened to 'tumbling strains of Aboriginal chant'.[52] Let's focus on this word Dreaming. C.P Mountford in the 1960s published a series of books of Aboriginal Dreamtime stories, which in many ways further established the Dreaming as in the public domain. Now quite a few composers have used the term, including Sculthorpe. For many Aboriginal people, the use of this word may very well be disrespectful. His note about his 'tumbling strains' shows other ways he referenced Indigenous music without drawing upon actual examples.

In examples 4–10 below the names of the composers have been withheld.

Example 4: Ulpirra (1993). The composer states: '*Ulpirra* is an Aboriginal word meaning pipe or flute.' The very general phrase 'an Aboriginal word for' homogenises the diversity of Aboriginal peoples and their cultures. It is also a little romantic, and the lives of many Indigenous people are far from romantic.

Example 5: Binyang (1996). The composer states: '*Binyang* means bird in the now defunct Sydney Aboriginal language'. Ouch! That's my language. In fact, it never was wholly defunct given the many *Dharug* words that are in use in Australian English (e.g. cooee, corroboree, wallaby, wombat, and more). As well, language reclamation is ongoing in many regions of the South-East. The Sydney language, and related neighbouring languages, are now being taught in some community and tertiary sectors in Sydney. The year 2019 is the International Year of Indigenous Languages and such simplistic use of Indigenous language in music composition needs to be more considered and/or revised.

Example 6: Impressions from the Dreamtime: a suite for solo guitar (1988). The composer states:

> *These pieces, as their title suggests, are not program-matic, but impressions or feelings about various legends and myths from the Dreamtime of the*

*Australian Aborigines. The musical language is
my own and it was not my intention to mimic in
any way, any aspect of their rich culture; rather
I have simply used these stories as a starting point
for my own fantasies.*

The movements include: I. The legend of fire, II. Frog
dreaming, III. *Kondole* and the corroboree, IV. The black
swan, V. Finale: The dancers are changed into animals.
It's an early work by the composer, and although
couched in respectful tone, the appropriateness of the
title and meaning could still be ambivalent.

Example 7: Mularra Lament: for solo guitar (1999). On
the AMC website the composer states that this piece:

> *uses a fragment of an indigenous songline as a
> way of exploring ideas of reconciliation. It craves
> atonement and expresses sorrow for past wrongs.*
> Mularra *also examines a theme central to indig-
> enous culture, that in death, the full richness of
> artistic life is celebrated, hence there are sections of
> dance-like exhilaration as well as mourning. The
> piece is in three main sections: an opening statement
> of the songline, a ritual celebratory dance and a
> third solemn and sparse lament.*

It is not clear whether the songline he uses is his own
invention or Indigenous. If the latter, we need to know
whose songline it is and where from. Is it for public
airing? Was permission obtained to use it? If so, is
permission still current? Why wasn't such permission

mentioned by the composer? If it was his invention it needs to be stated clearly. Even the word 'songline' may need addressing.

Example 8: Parardi: for viola and piano (1988). The composer states: '*Parardi* is the *Walpiri* word for rainbow.' What's wrong with the word rainbow? Indigenous culture is not folk culture. It's not a resource for public use. If the composer received permission to use this word, or if it is sufficiently in the public domain, then the composer should state so in his short overview to the piece.

Example 9: Yunggamurra—river spirit (1984). The composer states that this piece:

> *is a setting of prose and verse by the Australian writer Patricia Wrightson, O.B.E. She responded to my request for permission to set some of her work by extracting the following from her book,* The Dark Bright Water, *which was first published in 1979 by the Hutchinson Publishing Group Limited. I had made a long search for material to set and I was delighted with the above text provided by Patricia Wrightson, to do with spirits of Aboriginal myth and legend. Her images spark a strong response and were a challenge to me. Her work is subtle, mysterious, suggesting for example the* Yunggamurra *as both river spirit and aboriginal woman.*

Wrightson was an Australian writer who at times drew

upon Aboriginal mythology. Here a composer has collaborated with an author, yet the author used Indigenous culture as a resource.

Example 10: The concert event '*Ulpirra Sonatines*—Australian and French Flute Music', was given on 9 March 2016 in the Melbourne Recital Centre. Melissa Doecke and Mark Isaacs presented a program from their new CD *Ulpirra Sonatines*. This is an example of both an advertised programmed concert event and a CD release sustaining the use of an Indigenous word that might risk offence.

At this stage I would like to qualify that while there is remedial work to do, many of these composers are doing that work today. And Indigenous musicians and artists can also at times be in breach of what is culturally appropriate as well.[53]

Examples of respectful engagements

It must be stated that the following are just two examples where composers are engaged meaningfully with Indigenous peoples. It in no way diminishes others by omission.

Example 11: Mark Pollard's *Gunnai Dreaming* (2009) is 'inspired by one of the creation dreaming stories of the *Gunnai* people. It begins with the sound of the bullroarer and the depiction of landscape and local animals spoken and sung in *Gunnai* language'. At Eora College and among my people we don't use the bullroarer as an instrument. This is the case for most Aboriginal peoples.

It is not a publicly displayed cultural piece, but a sacred object for use in men's ceremony. That aside, Pollard shows admirable engagement with the peoples whose story he uses—very much as equals. He states:

> *This work was developed in close consultation with the Lavalla Catholic Senior Choir and the Gunnai Indigenous community. [...] It uses reclaimed language of the Gunnai people. The elders of this community have kindly granted permission for the use of this text in this work [...] the spoken sections in traditional language should be where possible spoken by a Koori.'*

Example 12: In several of his works, composer and jazz musician Kevin Hunt has worked with Aboriginal people in genuine collaboration. They contribute to his actual compositions, shaping the rehearsal process in ways he didn't envisage, even improvising on his pieces mid-performance, which may stem from Indigenous traditions. He has shared many a gig with Indigenous people and so from the inside knows the rhythmic idiosyncrasies that can and do occur. He lives a life with Aboriginal people, which is well beyond any project specifications, and conducts himself with a great sense of humility. He's been engaged in this way for around 25 to 30 years. He therefore also adapts and remains fluid in the realisation of his works with Indigenous performers.

Recommendations for composers who are referencing

Indigenous music, culture, themes and narratives are listed in chapter four. These will serve as a guide for current and future work in this arena, and also as a guide for composers wishing to make adjustments to their past works.

3: Hearing the Ngarra-burria sound

The *Ngarra-burria* First Peoples Composers program had three precedents.

The Eora Centre's Contemporary Aboriginal Performers of 1994 included music students and staff working with the theatre students and staff, under the direction of well-known Aboriginal theatre director Noel Tovey. During the year we staged incidental music to theatre shows, and also one new-music concert, each with repeated performances. Some of the works for the concert were based on experiences of incarceration by two of the musician members of the group. Under Tovey's direction and staging it was a powerful performance. I was the main composer-facilitator and used a lot of open form scoring and graphics to facilitate access for some 'non-reader' musicians. This worked well and also allowed each member of the group to contribute to the real-time composition of the piece in a communal way. In our composition sessions at times the *Ngarra-burria* composers also look at non-traditional notation methods.

Opera Ochre was a short-lived contemporary music project that a few Sydney musicians formed in 1999,

spearheaded by opera singer Jeffrey Locke. He came to
the Eora Centre and met with Darryl Griffen (soon-to-
be College Director) and me. Together we co-wrote and
staged an operatic cantata—*Songs of Hope and Reflection,*
with rock, jazz and new music in the mix. Performers
included three chorus members of the Australian Opera
company where Locke was based, Sydney jazz musicians Cameron Undy, Jeremy Borthwick and Michael
Brown, string players Tony Jones and Vanessa Chalker,
Indigenous members included Ian Callen (drums and
percussion), Rachel Nehanda Woods (voice), Darryl
(voice and co-composer), myself (jazz guitar and
co-composer) and New Guinean musician Michael
Hibberd (percussion). As well, Stephen Lalor conducted
and played piano, and the film lecturer at the Eora
Centre, Elena Guest, produced the event. We called
upon Jimmy Little to be the MC for the one concert
we gave, which was at the Sydney Conservatorium.
Deborah Cheetham was soon to form an opera company
on a much larger scale, and sustain the energy!

The premiere of the 'Our Music, Performing Place,
Listening to Sydney' day unfolded at the Sydney
Conservatorium of Music Faculty of Sydney University
on 30 June 2012. It was produced by Conservatorium
jazz staff member Kevin Hunt, and Julia Torpey, an
Aboriginal ANU PhD candidate. I had brought to the
then Dean, Professor Kim Walker, Indigenous music
in Sydney that was mostly less heard, and that needed
support. After that Kevin and I gathered about fifteen
Indigenous musicians together from his sources, and

also mine at Eora. These included Davina Captain, Jacinta Tobin, Clarence Slockee, Richard Green, Charlie Trindall, Sandra Spalding, Peter McKenzie, Matthew Doyle, Karen Smith, Mary Daniels, Marlene Cummins, Vic Simms, Brenda Gifford, Matt Ferguson, and more. Most attended a meeting at the Conservatorium prior to the performance day—which Kevin believed to be the first large gathering of contemporary Indigenous musicians at the Conservatorium in its history. Kevin and Julia developed a program and a template for the event.

Everybody received payment for their performances, which, given Australia's frequent deference to Indigenous cultural contribution, was an important aspect of the event. I participated in some performances and gave one presentation on my compositions. Kevin acknowledged me in the program as a founder, given my input and the related work I'd been doing over the years. Kevin performed his compositions, including interpretations of three *Dharug* traditional songs with Clarence Slockee, Richard Green and Matthew Doyle. This was new music/jazz meeting Sydney's oldest music tradition, facilitated by Indigenous musicians and Kevin, in mutually respectful collaboration. The day still unfolds bi-annually.

Your *Ngarra-burria*: First Peoples Composers

Earlier, in the quotation from the AMC website, I mentioned the names of the five composer participants in the program from late 2016 to late 2018. Once again these included Rhyan Clapham (*Murrawarri* and *Ngemba*), Brenda Gifford (*Dhurga*), Tim Gray (*Gumbaynggirr* and *Wiradjuri*), Troy Russell (*Gamiliroi* and *Biripi*) and Elizabeth Sheppard (*Noongar Yamatji*).

From the outset John Davis from the AMC, Moogahlin Performing Arts co-artistic director Fred Copperwaite and I had conceived of goals for the program and the composers. These were:

> *hanging out and sensing the possibilities, acquiring new skills and the utilisation of these in new works that enabled the articulation of cultural context with more clarity, knowledge exchanges with all partners, and connecting with the new music scene.*

Claire Edwards from Ensemble Offspring also made valuable contributions to the development and realisation of these goals along the way. They were further shaped by the composers, especially in relation to personal Indigenous experience and some current trajectories such as language reclamation. After observing some of the music in rehearsals, Fred noted that these new works were a shift in paradigms of expression and artfulness for our emerging composer-musicians.

John saw the possibility for real inroads and impact upon the new music and classical cultural sectors, and confirmed it was 'about time'. These responses suggest real outcomes—tangible ways that the *Ngarra-burria* composers can be heard, and potentially owned by Australian music lovers.

I was simply happy that each composer had made a start. When teaching at the Eora Centre, I had learned that small steps were just as much worth celebrating as major achievements, and for individuals, could be major achievements in themselves. Back in 2016, until we had seen the first drafts of the first compositions, as mentors Kevin Hunt and I had wondered whether all would manage, and quite expected that one or two would pull out. This was because composition was an additional commitment on top of their course work, earning a living and other music, family and community obligations. After we heard the emerging pieces in the first workshop with Ensemble Offspring in 2017, both of us recognised that they were there to stay. The pieces sounded very much like they had a future, and the composers were stoked up from the workshop. After that first workshop with the group we also realised that each composer had their own method of approach, subtlety of style, nuance of expression, themes they were exploring—and sound. I call it fingerprints.

Establishing an entry level

After rehearsing a long section of a new work, *Murrawarri* composer Rhyan Clapham remarked: 'It's sounding close.' I love the audacity of this comment from a young Aboriginal musician to one of Australia's leading contemporary chamber groups—Ensemble Offspring. This comment also suggests something about the intended level of the *Ngarra-burria* program.

The program is for established Indigenous musicians to further refine their skills and experience new genres such as art music and jazz.[54] One has to be able to read music to enter the program, and to have composed and/or scored some music. It is for those who have more to explore, quite outside of blues, rock, reggae or country music. All who come into the program are really quite experienced, with some seasoned professionals from those styles too. We put a call out through the Eora Centre, through Aboriginal musicians we knew, through the AMC, through Moogahlin Performing Arts, and through Michael Hutchings—Indigenous officer with APRA. This was limited to NSW, to keep it localised and therefore manageable. Given our stipulation for established or experienced Indigenous musicians we knew that most applicants would be older musicians. Rhyan Clapham was 27 years old, the others were between their 40s and 70s. This experience and maturity transferred quickly to the articulation of their own sound. It was intentional on my part to attract and involve Indigenous professionals in the program, as they would enrich it from the start, and were likely to succeed and connect with the new music sector sooner. This proved to be the case.

In 2018, under the mentorship of Kim Cunio, Rhyan was working on a new piece, *Talk to Me I'm Listening*. By this stage he had previously completed a degree with a performance major in jazz drumming at UNSW, and was a rapper and songwriter with a good profile. In rehearsal it became clear to all of us that he had a remarkable sense of rhythmic intricacy. After the rehearsal I mentioned to him that a particularly complex iso-rhythm in the piece worked very well—a three-beat against a five-beat pattern in the two hands of the piano, which yielded shifting metrical emphases. He responded with: 'Yes, there's a few layers in it. I wanted another layer there too, a further three against five on the other instruments, in quick succession on the heels of the first, but I don't think they'd get it.' This is an example of just how complex this young composer's conceptions can be. Of course the group would have got it, but the example does point out his considerable skills. Deadly, eh! Above and beyond this, the musical experience that he himself engenders when working with musicians on his composition is one of sharing in a spirit of humility. We all felt that.

Rhyan's rhythmic ability resonates with the adaptable and fluid nature of rhythm in some Indigenous music contexts. My own perception of the complexities of this was not always so enlightened. In rehearsals in my 20s when I heard our musicians drop a beat in order to usher in the next phrase sooner, I would be annoyed, assuming it was wrong. I would ask to re-run the section of the song or piece. Yet on the next time through this rhythmic fluidity, resulting in truncating a phrase, or lengthening a note, often occurred at a different point. Over time I noticed that this trait occurred in various Indigenous music styles. I softened, learned to listen more acutely, and realised the beauty coursing through such approaches to performance. It is very natural and related to a life that many Indigenous people live—a life that is necessarily adaptable and fluid. In the *Ngarraburria* program I began to hear that Rhyan's and also Troy's rhythmic sense was both inventive and organic. It may or may not stem from their Indigenous life, but I suspect that at least in part it does.

4. Putting First Peoples first: cultural agency

In November 2018, during the recordings at the School of Music at the ANU, the ensemble, the composers, John Davis, the engineers and I faced a dilemma. We wanted a professional product, yet at times the professionalism got in the way. Members of the ensemble highlighted that the recording could have been better, and even aspects of the performance—better 'takes'— but there had been limited time. Claire Edwards, artistic director for Ensemble Offspring, was absent at the time of the recordings. She emailed to say that perhaps the recording shouldn't be released until all partners were satisfied with the product. It was certainly valid. Later, after the recordings, some of the composers, Fred—a *Bunuba* man— and myself met, and talked about this matter of delaying a release or airplay. For our part, we were happy to send the mixed and mastered recordings to the ABC for broadcast, or to a CD manufacturer for pressing. Some partners were not totally satisfied. It was certainly sounding very good, but not yet optimum. At length the composers, Fred and I, drilled down to the fact that within the *Ngarra-burria* program there is the matter of where cultural agency sits. As Aboriginal members in the project, and as an Indigenous-led initiative we agreed that cultural agency sat with us, and that this should help to resolve any hard decisions. Fred simply stated: 'First Peoples first.' It reverberated around the room.

We all agreed that the members of the ensemble were empathetic in their engagement with Indigenous music and musicians—wholly so—yet we had to assume cultural agency and lead. We knew the program had some significance and we felt that the matter of cultural agency needed to be made known and heard more broadly. The context of this paper facilitates that in part. At the time of writing this, Kim Cunio is still to do the final mix and mastering of the recordings, and we're yet to present them to all partners. We will negotiate a way forward from there.

Fred—a leader in the Indigenous cultural arts sector, with a depth and breadth of understanding and experience—also tabled 'the difference between excellence and relevance'. He highlighted that the recent recordings and indeed the whole program was foremost about relevance, and that excellence was desirable but not the mitigating factor over and above relevance. It tied in nicely with the First Peoples first resolution.

At times significant cultural matters are being explored and expressed in and through these new Indigenous music recordings. This includes: Indigenous historical matters, common Indigenous themes or issues, composer's family histories, language reclamation, and more. Indeed, some of the works contain a depth of symbolism that is articulated through the actual dots (the notation) and later captured in the recording. If, in the short term, the recordings were held back while we met again and aimed for excellence, we might be delaying the hearing of new Indigenous voices. So the relevance-versus-excellence resolution will apply in future editions of the program. This too needs to be heard. Such guiding principles we slowly came to through the course of the program. All partners are the richer for it, and we couldn't have arrived there without any of them.

I believe that the composers, Fred, John Davis, Claire, the musicians, the mentors and myself, have been a part of something that has developed Indigenous music, and that Australian music on the whole has moved forward via the program. And until this time, most new music events in Australia that had an Indigenous element had been led by non-Indigenous professionals. Here we conceived of something led by Indigenous people—Moogahlin Performing Arts staff and myself were turning things around. This is not wholly new: our classical organisations and musicians, working under the umbrella of an Indigenous music or performing arts organisation, and under Indigenous 'classical' musicians' leadership—more in our domain and addressing similarly our approaches and expressions.[55] But it has become essential to be in a leadership role in the expression of our music, culture, themes and narratives. In fact, we are obliged in this regard to our families and our communities.

The first precedent had been Deborah Cheetham's Short Black Opera Company, established in 2008—an Indigenous-led initiative. Her focus at present is on the training of talented Indigenous people for performance in choral and opera settings, particularly her own compositions, and bringing Victorian Indigenous history to light through music. Deborah's conception of what is possible in the arena of Indigenous music is second to none, and she has also recently started the 'One Day in January' series—an Indigenous chamber orchestra that meets each January (and will at other times of the year as well). Deborah is also a part-time mentor for the *Ngarra-burria* composers in 2019. As I hear it, the work of the Black Arm Band could be mistaken for being similar to both the Short Black Opera and to *Ngarra-burria*, but their music has a different purpose and is much more in a social and commercial vein, at times engaging classical performers. It isn't new music or classical, nor is their work about training and the development of musicians.

5. The mentoring process

It's not often that one gains an inside view of what unfolds in Indigenous and non-Indigenous music collaborations, so the following episodes serve to enable us to 'hear' the interactions in rehearsal and performance as closely as is possible.

Ensemble Offspring and local musicians at Brewarrina

In April 2018 Ensemble Offspring and the composers visited Brewarrina in north-western NSW to perform in the *Baiame's Ngunnhu* Festival. Lily Shearer, *Murrawarri* and *Ngemba* woman, and co-artistic director of Moogahlin Performing Arts with Fred, comes from the Bre' community, and was the Festival Director. This is a festival centred on the shores of the Barwon-Darling River and overlooking the ancient Brewarrina fish traps, made in ancient times by local Aboriginal people. The Friday evening opened with a corroboree, and at one stage everybody was invited into the corroboree ground to participate. Some of the members of Ensemble Offspring, Kim Cunio and the composers made the most of the opportunity. It was a beautiful moment! The invitation to participate in a local corroboree is a true expression of welcome and inclusion.

On the Saturday, music concerts started in the morning and ran all day. Ensemble Offspring were scheduled at about 4pm, and a moderate crowd of about 60 gathered close to listen. Afterwards I spoke to many of the local elders, who said that they liked it, that it was different, but in truth they weren't 'bowled over'. Yet the Bre' kids loved it—a large wriggly bunch right under the ensemble's noses. They were particularly intrigued with Claire Edwards' vibraphone and two of them decided to join her on stage, even adding a note here or there. I sensed that she valued this shared performance just as much as when performing with the Sydney Symphony Orchestra. One thing we all gleaned from their playing was that this was their place. It was still primarily their space when we visited with our show. Upon spotting some friends down at the river, some of the kids listening simply got up and walked right through the stage mid-performance. They were impressive—they knew and owned their river and its environs. We were the visitors.

The next day Glen Skuthorpe sang. Glen is a country-rock and roots singer originally from the Bre' and nearby Goodooga region, yet is now an international star based partly in Canada. Glen has great craft and real depth. Compared to the previous day, the audience doubled in numbers, to over 100, and this caught my attention. Where were they yesterday? The reason was the simple fact that the locals loyally supported their own Indigenous musicians, perhaps more so than other Indigenous musicians.[56] We all felt fine about this, it was, in fact, good and right. After Glen, another local performed—elder statesman of country music, Col Hardy. Once again the audience doubled, with over 200 people sitting to hear him play. We couldn't compete, and again this satisfied us, because the sense of local pride was palpable. We were perhaps too left-of-centre too. One of the composers later shared with me a Facebook post from a local that said words to the effect of, 'classical music is not our music'. None of us minded, it was only one comment, and in the year since, Rhyan has kept up a closer association with elders there, and we've been invited back. I hear Jimmy's words once again: 'We all have our part to play.' So, whether the whole audience supports it or not, is fine.

A mentor at work

At the Eora Centre in May 2018 we had a workshop with the ensemble on the new works in progress. Midway through Troy Russell's *Where Are You?* piece, Roland Peelman spun around at the piano, and challenged him: 'What do you intend by this chord?' and, 'This note here must mean something, I can't see what it is here for.' Troy couldn't quite answer. He is a good composer, but obviously felt placed on the spot, unprepared to respond to the probing of a professional musician. Kim Cunio and I as composer mentors were just happy that the piece was at a suitable level to workshop. I offered an answer: 'Play the dots as they are again, then we can discuss other options.' In a break I mentioned to Troy that Roland's delving into the meaning of the dots was something that he does with and for the benefit of any composer. Troy 'got on board' with this after the break, and was more prepared to account for his notation both musically and in the way it related to his concept or story. Most Indigenous composers are not yet used to working with professional classical or new music musicians.

The composer's rights

Later in the workshop, while playing through Elizabeth Sheppard's *Buradowi* song, Roland stopped and asked her to tell him the purpose of a particular phrase, and also whether the orchestration could be made more transparent in some sections. She suggested that she should speak to local elders of the *Dharug* language she was using, as any changes might emphasise aspects of the lyrics in new ways, to which Roland responded: 'No. I want to hear from you as the composer!' They went back and forth on this for a while. However, Kim and I affirmed that Roland was indeed correct. If permission was given to use the language, then Elizabeth did not really need to be deferring to the elders on matters of craft or artful expression. In talking with Elizabeth later, it was clear that she also now understood this. At times in the music arena, I've observed that we place elders under unnecessary pressures, engaging them in artistic matters or mechanical concerns when they'd rather focus on other aspects of their contribution to an initiative or an event, like a Welcome or a speech, or simply to be present and included.

Women's participation

Back in the mid-2017 workshop with the ensemble at Eora, Brenda Gifford's *Gambambara* had been played through. She had included a clapstick pulse consistently through a later section of the piece and there followed discussion about it sounding 'too insistent, that perhaps it should come out'. Brenda glanced sideways at me. I asked her if she wanted it in, which she did. Yet still some discussion continued to the effect of 'it's too much'. Brenda and I spoke, and I instructed: 'Play it as is.' Later Brenda shared her objection with the other Indigenous composers, saying: 'It's important for Indigenous women to be able to play the clapsticks, as that's one instrument that in the old times we played. We are not to be shut out.' She was writing Indigenous women's enablement into the work. It was a relevance-versus-excellence issue. Relevance won, and the clapsticks have always stayed in, just as she intended—to symbolise women's traditions of participation. Later she shared this with the ensemble too.

As Indigenous musicians collaborating with a

non-Indigenous group, all of this may be going on and more, of which many present may not even be aware—whether Indigenous or not. It's a negotiation process, and in the end it results in cultural growth for all participating.

Composing in two languages

Yoora Tattoo is a movement from *Kooranginy Suite* by Elizabeth Sheppard, an elder of the group. She uses two languages in all of her titles—her Indigenous language and English, representing the two strands of her life and their coming together. It is also emblematic of reconciliation. *Yoora* means 'clapsticks' in her language, and tattoo pertains to the drums of military groups. She couples them into one voice in her title, representing two traditions of music making. To quote from Elizabeth, she 'composes expressive music on Indigenous themes [i.e. stories], and juxtaposes and interweaves symbolic motifs', in this instance, the interactions between two cultures in 1788. Her scores are delightfully decorative and contain many verbal prompts that draw us in. The various symbolic motifs are highlighted when they appear.

One of the things this piece by Elizabeth highlights is that Aboriginal people from all over Australia have a relationship with the place of the first colonisation of Australia, and stories there—the land of the *Dharug* speakers of Sydney.

Language reclamation

Rhyan Clapham is engaged in the process of his Indigenous language reclamation, and from the first meeting of the composers in late 2016 asked: 'Can we use voices?' In the Aboriginal language of the *Murrawarri* people of Brewarrina (the language of Rhyan's people), *Pitara Yaan Muru-wariki* means '*Murrawarri* is good, sweet talk.' He says: 'This is [the title of my piece] and the goal of my composition. The work represents both the strength of Indigenous language and the journey of acquiring this knowledge.' However, the program had given the composers an instrumental ensemble to work with. So we agreed that perhaps he might sing with them. Also I asked Lamorna Nightingale, flautist of Ensemble Offspring, to demonstrate talking or singing through the flute whilst playing. Rhyan latched onto this, and incorporated it meaningfully and artfully into his piece. In fact he went further than Kevin and I had envisioned.

In *Pitara Yaan Muru-wariki* Rhyan used four words that were assigned to the four instruments. These were: *Thirra* (meaning song) for flute; *Pintanj* (meaning tongue) for clarinet; *Paliputharran* (lungs) for cello and, lastly, *Milkakari* ('someone with no ears'/a non-listener) which was assigned to the vibraphone. The vibraphone part is scored to play consistently in some sections of the work, seemingly oblivious to the other parts talking 'sweet *Murrawarri*'. Plausibly this is symbolic of the wider Australian voice and the Indigenous voice. He assigns the words inventively and artfully. They shape the melodic contours and rhythms of the four parts of the ensemble. He allows the performers firstly, and the listeners secondly, to engage with and participate in his language reclamation. This is humbling, the gift from the pen of a young Indigenous composer. It is also hugely significant—to invite us into the world of his current cultural narrative.[57]

An Acknowledgement to Country

In September 2017 I was invited to present to the International Association of Music Libraries conference at the National Library of Australia, in Canberra, and thought to use Troy Russell's piece *Nucoorilma* as an alternative to an Acknowledgement of Country. The following is an excerpt from my presentation.

> *From this point I want to acknowledge country, through playing a piece by one of the composers in the AMPlify Indigenous Composers Initiative. Nucoorilma—a piece by Troy Russell—means apple tree (in Gamillaroi language) and is about a physical and spiritual journey that Troy's great-grandmother took, near Tinga NSW, in the early 20th century. It was a long walk away from her own people's country, and with the man she loved. They were chaperoned by elders, and, along the way, there were apple trees that sustained*

them. In the new country the family and people of her husband-to-be welcomed her. So, inherent in this piece is a real-life practice of Welcome to Country. What really grabs my attention in this story and also in the music is the physical sense of the journey—of covering lots of ground, of looking for food along the way. This is reflected in the music: the opening ostinato suggests walking, and the floating flute phrase the open skies above. In many ways in the piece we can listen for these tangibly physical aspects of a Welcome to Country. So with Troy's permission I use Nucoorilma *as an acknowledgement of country here today.*

Nucoorilma is alive with family history and Aboriginal traditions. Troy is a composer who is particularly good at fostering in the audience something of the meaning of a piece through the piece itself. His intended communication through his music is very effective. In August 2018 he presented this piece to an undergraduate class in Contemporary Indigenous Music Studies at the School of Music at the ANU. Without providing any information, he asked them to listen to the piece, and later asked: 'What may it be about? What are you hearing?' Most students said it's about taking a journey. They were right. Only then did he amplify further detail about his people, his family, the journey in question and why the journey was necessary.

The pieces—content and cultural matters

Significantly, the five composers in the program always directed the cultural content of their works themselves. We as mentors were keenly aware of this fact. For instance, Aboriginal language reclamation is current, and right from the start we realised that there was a strong and relevant focus on language reclamation from some of the composers. There was also a focus on exploring family stories, the natural environment—from Aboriginal seasons to simple meditations by a river, interpretations of the colonial story of Sydney— and one composer, Tim Gray, created music for an imagined fantasy-thriller film that was a metaphor for his recovery from addiction.[58] Both Troy and Tim wrote at least one work that was not concerned with anything solely related to Indigenous culture or experience—just music itself. This shows that Indigenous culture and identity are not always the centrepiece in the creative works of an Indigenous person. In some instances, in some works, these composers just want to be known as composers. And at other times the context of being Indigenous is important to address.

In relation to the use of cultural materials, it was significant that none of the composers in the program drew on Aboriginal music, stories, language or instruments from anywhere other than their own language region. This contrasts with the way, as we now know, some non-Indigenous composers have referenced Aboriginal and Torres Strait Islander culture from across all of Australia. In my view individual pieces have not been enriched by it, but are the poorer. For Aboriginal people it is not our practice.

6: Thoughts and recommendations for the new music sector

Moogahlin Performing Arts staff Fred Copperwaite and Lily Shearer, John Davis and the AMC team, Ensemble Offspring, Michael Hutchings from APRA, the three mentors, Kevin Hunt, Kim Cunio, Deborah Cheetham and I, heads of department at the Eora Centre, ABC engineer Stephen Adams, composer and radio host Andrew Ford, believe that we can now gratefully say, after the first edition of *Ngarra-burria*, that the worth of the program has been validated.

Brenda has received several commissions, including from Ensemble Offspring and also the Canberra International Music Festival; and a Bundanon Arts residency. Troy has received funding for a residency at Blacktown Arts Centre to present his new works with choreography in a staged setting. Roland Peelman is considering a further opportunity. Rhyan won the Peter Sculthorpe Fellowship for 2018–19, and has also received a new commission from the Canberra Symphony Orchestra Australian Series for performers Claire Edwards and himself. Elizabeth, Tim, Brenda,

Troy and Rhyan have all received commissions from a consortium in Sydney. The Royal Australian Navy Band has come on board to support the 2019 edition program. The list goes on.

Some Indigenous musicians and other Indigenous people have gained employment working with non-Aboriginal composers. I don't suggest that anybody should stand in the way of that. We simply ask that a deeper long-term engagement be the working method. That is the hope for the *Ngarra-burria* composers.

We also have to move past the still-prevalent notion about working with 'authentic Aborigines' (noun intended) or authentic Aboriginal music or instruments. Projects need support even if the Indigenous people concerned don't necessarily speak their language, and where their culture is largely fractured. Indigenous people are as diverse today as the rest of the population. One of the composers in the program uses the term 'not black enough' to account for how at times, the local Indigenous people of the South-East are overlooked. People in the South-East have had equally authentic Aboriginal experiences, just different from those from the Red Centre or the far north. The Denis Byrne article raised the fact that authenticity was an issue for non-Indigenous people in NSW back in the early 1800s. Our heritage and identity are not for others to decide.

Another outcome has been facilitating meaningful experiences and fruitful connections between the *Ngarra-burria* composers and other musicians. These included ethnomusicologist Dr Bonnie McConnell and composer Dr Natalie Williams at the School of Music ANU, sound engineers Craig Greening and Matt Barnes, also at the School; Stephen Adams, composer and ABC engineer and producer, and more. In April 2017 we hosted a dinner in Canberra with William Barton and Bunna Lawrie, frontman of the band Coloured Stone. We were able to share our thoughts in a more relaxed setting, and afterwards paid a late night visit to the Aboriginal Tent Embassy. There, Bunna led us through a simple smoking ceremony. The composers and Bunna were particularly delighted at how non-Indigenous friends participated in the ceremony.

The anticipated outcome of all this work now is that in Australia our new music and classical sectors will rethink their obligations in this arena, and support the strategies in the recommendations below. For too long we've been complicit in facilitating non-Indigenous composers occupying the Indigenous space via Aboriginal referencing. I understand much of this activity, as in part it suggests that we are evolving in our collective identity as composers in this country, and that Indigenous culture is increasingly seen to be a large part of informing that evolution. Some of our composers may still need assistance in articulating exactly what they want to say on the page at times—in score format—yet, whilst in 2017 the need was common, in 2018 such required assistance was much less. This is a great outcome

There are education programs around Indigenous Cultural Awareness in many large institutions. I propose that they should be mandatory for any composer utilising Indigenous music or stories, without which they should not be commissioned and funded, nor scheduled for rehearsal, performance or broadcast. This is neither policing nor censoring. It is a recommendation to address cultural integrity for all parties. It keeps Indigenous cultural agency in the hands of Indigenous peoples. It is a recommendation for development.

We took a new intake of composers in February 2019, and very much look forward to working them through the year, and potentially into 2020. Once again the composers are already experienced musicians: they can read music, and each one wants to challenge themselves and participate in the new music and perhaps jazz sectors. The composers for 2019 are Marcus Corowa, Eric Avery, Sonya Holowell, Nardi Simpson and James Henry. Ensemble Offspring is taking more of a mentoring role around the composer-performer relationship in 2019, while the Royal Australian Navy Band Sydney (and its many ensembles) directed by Lieutenant Brian O'Kane, is the main partnering performance group for this year.

Recommendations

Our guidelines for the way forward are:

- Include us.
- Act not solely within the new music sector's terms of reference.

- Recognise that success is not dictated by those in places of entitlement.
- Remember when engaging with Indigenous peoples that cultural agency sits with them.
- Employ the relevance-versus-excellence template when working with Indigenous musicians.
- Remember that we still aim for excellence.

Acknowledge that:

- Many non-Indigenous composers have been using aspects of Indigenous music and culture, and Indigenous themes and narratives.
- We are shifting paradigms of expression within the Indigenous music sector, and this deserves recognition and support.
- We must identify and revise Indigenous referencing and Indigenous posturing practices.
- Indigenous people are diverse.

Reform current records and practices:

- Some works from deceased composers may require a foreword, or be framed in another way.[59]
- Ensure that our living composers are informed, and reframe works that have been inappropriately referenced as Indigenous

music, culture, themes or narratives, by way of a new foreword, or by negotiating permissions that should have been in place. They may also simply re-title such works.

- When working in this arena non-Indigenous and Indigenous musicians alike would do well to refer to the Australia Council's recommended *Protocols for Producing Australian Indigenous Music.*
- Get advice on the use of Indigenous words, stories or concepts in the so-called public domain.
- Consider the benefits of a long-term engagement with Aboriginal people versus a one-off collaboration for a commission.

Money

Our major music organisations need to revise their allocation of time and money.[60] You and your organisation, whether large or small, can:

- Fund, commission, program and profile Indigenous composers.
- Pay what is fair. Given the fact that many non-Indigenous composers have earned solid commission fees while referencing Indigenous music and culture, our composers deserve to be paid similar fees, not a 'less experienced composer' rate.

- Hang out with us, you are most welcome. Don't just do the gig and run.[61]
- Talk with Indigenous composers and Indigenous peoples about any potential project.
- Get to know the Moogahlin Performing Arts staff by attending Moogahlin events.
- Speak with Claire Edwards and the members of Ensemble Offspring who have worked closely with the *Ngarra-burria* composers for two years. Also speak with Kevin Hunt.

'Everyone has a part to play' (Jimmy Little).

Endnotes

1. New music can be defined as scored contemporary music stemming from the classical or experimental traditions.

2. In fact the family descends from Sydney's Aboriginal people, but had left Sydney about 1835, not to return for 80 years.

3. www.records.nsw.gov.au/agency/560

4. www.bniproject.com/history

5. Indigenous Australian groups are called by their language.

6. Once again I emphasise that there exist different views for the people and their language in Sydney and its surrounds. The Norman Tindale map of Australian Indigenous languages (1974) highlights the Hawkesbury River basin as the land of the *Dharug*, and which includes Western Sydney, the Blue Mountains, much of Sydney, the Hawkesbury and much of the Central Coast. Eastern Sydney was listed as *Kameraigal* on his original map. The term *Eora* didn't factor. See http://www.sl.nsw.gov.au/sites/default/files/4790_indigenous_services_-_a3_collection_item_updated6final.pdf Accessed 5 March 2019.

7. The Eora Centre is an Indigenous College that is part of TAFE NSW. It runs programs from certificates to advanced diplomas in a range of disciplines, and at times degrees in partnership with external universities.

8. He had also been one of the interview panel who had recommended me for my appointment.

9   Brenda Croft, *Future Directions of Indigenous Research Lecture*, ANU 2018.

10   http://press-files.anu.edu.au/downloads/press/p72561/pdf/article0414.pdf, p83.Accessed 12 Feb 2019.

11   Dr Liza-Mare Syron 'Letterbox-gate' in Anita Heiss, *Growing Up Aboriginal in Australia, Carlton,* Vic: Black Inc., 2018, p.225.

12   Name withheld.

13   I finished school in 1980 and didn't study full-time until 1984 when I entered a Diploma of Music at the Northern Rivers College of Advanced Education, Lismore—a largely forgotten powerhouse of arts and music education in our older tertiary system. (Most now do not know what a CAE was.)

14   In a later section on precedents to the *Ngarra-Burria* program I will look at aspects of this.

15   The theatre directors at Eora at the time were Howard Jackson (playwright) and Aboriginal theatre director Noel Tovey. They too assisted in fostering this student experience marvellously.

16   See http://www.moogahlin.org/

17   The Centre moved from Redfern to nearby Chippendale in 1993.

18   Here I am using *Dharug* as a generic and inclusive term for the language of Sydney.

19   Ensemble Offspring, the leading performing partner group in the initiative, have been centrepiece to the Indigenous composers of *Ngarra-Burria*, assisting them in finding a place in this new musical terrain. With them we have workshopped, rehearsed and recorded. We've dined together,

laughed together, wrestled a little, and ultimately I suggest that together we've brought Australian music forward.

20   Truncated version from Australian Music Centre website, accessed 10 Dec 2018.
https://www.abc.net.au/classic/new-waves/amplify_indigenous-composer-initiative/9225024

21   Graeme Skinner, ed. *The Composer Speaks.* Sydney: Sounds Australia, 1991.

22   So-called Indigenous issues are wider Australian issues, and although the term is useful for quick reference, it is inadequate and polarising.

23   Graeme Skinner.

24   Skinner.

25   Skinner.

26   My PhD was titled 'Working as a Regionalist Composer'. To my view, whilst it wasn't very good, there was something in it.

27   Performances, awards and commissions.

28   Later I did do a Masters and also a PhD through the Conservatorium Faculty of Sydney University, yet at a respectable distance, spending very little time there as per my work requirements and personal needs.

29   Note that above, I esteem Sculthorpe as significant. But for a few reasons he has never been one that I listen to much, and in no way has he influenced my music, unlike his influence on many Australian composers.

30   I did like the way he was always proud of his lighter works as well as his more serious works.

31   Name withheld.

32   I know or have known all of these, except oddly, given my involvement, I never met David Page.

33   McCallum reviewed the work in *The Australian* 13 September 2016 but confined himself to an account of the performance, with the exception of the closing sentence: 'The stolen generations has become a central story in contemporary Australia and this telling, by a member of that generation, goes to the heart of our sense of self.'

34   John Davis, personal interview, 11 Feb 2019.

35   https://aiatsis.gov.au/explore/articles/indigenous-australi-ans-aboriginal-and-torres-strait-islander-people

36   Ruth A. Firor *Folkways in Thomas Hardy* New York: Perpetua Edition 1962.

37   Bruce Pascoe *Dark Emu* Broome: Western Australia, Magabala Books, 2014.

38   Indigenism is a term that Pascoe uses referring to a sustainable lifestyle alternative to capitalism.

39   'Much has yet to be learned about our Aboriginal music', *The Sydney Morning Herald*. 18 April 1950. p.2. http://nla.gov.au/nla.news -article27574952

40   It's not every Australian composer who gets to study with an Australian mid-20th century great 20 years the senior of both Peter Sculthorpe and Larry Sitsky.

41   I was 21 or 22 when studying with Penberthy.

42   James Murdoch, Melbourne: Sun Books 1975.

43   Jonathan Paget, 'Has Sculthorpe Misappropriated Indigenous Melodies? In *Musicology Australia*, Volume 35, 2013—Issue 1: Contemporary Approaches to Transcultural Music Research in Australia and New Zealand, pp. 86–111.

44   I refer to the iconic photograph by Mervyn Bishop of Prime

Minister Gough Whitlam in 1975 pouring a handful of sand into the hands of the traditional owner, Vincent Lingiari, on Gurindji lands NT.

45 As far as I'm aware he never made this public.

46 The Australia Council, *Protocols for Producing Indigenous Australian Music*, 2007, is a benchmark guide in this field. https://www.australiacouncil.gov.au/workspace/uploads/files/music-protocols-for-indigenous-5b4bfc140118d.pdf

47 Bruce Chatwin, *The Songlines*. Ringwood, Vic: Penguin Books, 1988.

48 See www.australianmusiccentre.com.au

49 Note: I'm not assuming anything in this sphere. I've met many of them, but more importantly they present no profile of themselves as being Indigenous.

50 See Australian Music Centre website for the composer's notes about the piece.

51 AMC website.

52 Liner notes to the CD recording, *Sculthorpe Requiem*, ABC Classics, 2005.

53 I've seen a few examples of this during my time as a Head of Department at the Eora Centre.

54 The program is not for Indigenous singer-songwriters who in other ways have their needs met by TAFEs, private music schools and contemporary music festivals.

55 These cannot be simply listed, yet many are contained within the breadth of this paper.

56 Rhyan Clapham's people are from near to Bre' and so he found quite a bit of support with his rap show as well.

57 Rhyan submitted this piece along with other pieces for the Create NSW Peter Sculthorpe Music Fellowship of 2018–19.

He also submitted a well-structured application, and won the scholarship.

58 Tim has given me permission to use this information.

59 I do not believe any Australian works should be censored or taken off the shelves. Yet further information could assist around the circumstances or era in which some works were written.

60 I refer to major music organisations in Australia, such as our six state-based symphony orchestras, the ABC, Music Viva, our fine chamber orchestras, Opera Australia and our other opera companies, other metropolitan orchestras, our leading new music small ensembles, our university resident ensembles, and more.

61 Much transpires in the Indigenous space when people spend time off project, hanging out. It always improves the engagement and the project. Such was the composers and Ensemble Offspring's experience in Brewarrina in 2018.

COPYRIGHT INFORMATION

PLATFORM PAPERS
Quarterly essays from Currency House Inc.
Founding Editor: Dr John Golder
Editor: Katharine Brisbane

Currency House Inc. is a non-profit association and resource centre advocating the role of the performing arts in public life by research, debate and publication.

Postal address: PO Box 2270, Strawberry Hills, NSW 2012, Australia
Email: info@currencyhouse.org.au Tel: (02) 9319 4953
Website: www.currencyhouse.org.au Fax: (02) 9319 3649

Editorial Committee: Katharine Brisbane AM, Michael Campbell, Doctor Julian Meyrick, Martin Portus, Dr Nick Shimmin, Dr Liza-Mare Syron.

NGARRA-BURRIA: New music and the search for an Australian Sound
© Christopher Sainsbury, 2019

ISBN 978-0-6484265-2-3
ISSN 1449-583X

Typeset in Garamond
Printed by Ligare Book Printers, Riverwood, NSW
Production by Currency Press Pty Ltd

FORTHCOMING

PP No.60, August 2019

CAPTURING THE VANISHING: A CHOREOGRAPHER AND FILM

Sue Healey

Dance is difficult to pin down. The potency of dance lies in its impermanence, its transient expression of life. By its very nature fleeting, it is not easily documented, notated, or archived, to secure it against oblivion. Dance is constantly shape-shifting, re-constructing and re-negotiating its mutability, which is, of course, its magic. This ephemerality presents paradoxes and survival challenges for Australian independent choreographers. Sue Healey, one of Australia's most admired and internationally acclaimed dancers and choreographers, has grappled with the problem for many years, experimenting with film and the moving image to capture the vanishing. This paper gives insight into her hazardous journey from the 1980s to the present, which produced great advances in technology and starkly diminishing resources for dance-making. Healey outlines her personal strategy for survival as employing a second medium—film. Can something new come from re-imagining the power of the human body through the medium of film? How can film capture the visceral reality of live performance, and take us beyond that vanishing point? Her adventures with dance-film give an insight.

AT YOUR LOCAL BOOKSHOP FROM 1 AUGUST

AND AS A PAPERBACK OR ONLINE

FROM OUR WEBSITE AT

WWW.CURRENCYHOUSE.ORG.AU